Seraph Creative is a collective of artists, writers, theologians & illustrators who desire to see the body of Christ grow into full maturity, walking in their inheritance as Sons of God on the Earth.

Sign up to our newsletter to know about future exciting releases.

Visit our website : www.seraphcreative.org

You Belong – A Children's Story

Written by Joey LeTourneau

Illustrations created by Galilee LeTourneau using MidJourney AI

Published by Seraph Creative in 2025

United States / United Kingdom / South Africa / Australia

www.seraphcreative.org

ISBN: 978-1-964959-66-5

eBook ISBN: 978-1-964959-67-2

Mama Giraffe was walking through the market one day, the sights around her bustling, familiar and all too gray.

3

There was much to do, and much to give. And the world of need didn't want to give an inch.

Busyness began to push her, and distractions always tried...

...but in her spirit rose that lifelong reminder that God's lost kids were all around her so that she could help find them.
And that's when she heard a little one's cries.

She turned from her path and dropped her list for another matter, where was this little one whose heart sounded so tattered?

Around the bend and tucked in a corner,
the young elephant shivered
with nothing to adorn her.

So, Mama bent down and out of her sack,
pulled a blanket and bread to fill
the little elephant's lack.

Half a smile crept up her long, gray face,
but still her hope sat with her, surrounded by
waste. Mama knew what she needed most, she
bent down with a whisper and drew extra close.

"You are loved, a daughter of the King.
Your life has more value than any of
these things. I would like to call you
one of our own, you belong to Papa
God, His light and treasure inside you
are what I've been shown."

Little Ellie jumped up spry, like one who had eaten a big banana cream pie. Her eyes lit up, her hope was full mast, this word softly spoken had filled her heart tank up fast.

With Mama, she walked through her shopping that day, until Ellie saw the young cheetah begging for food and had nothing to pay.

She took half the loaf she was just given, bent down towards his ear and gave a whisper that made this young cheetah quite smitten.

"You are loved, a child of the King. Your life has more value than any of these things. I would like to call you one of our own, you belong to Papa God, His light and treasure inside you are what I've been shown."

"What did you say?" Mama Giraffe asked. "I simply shared your whisper, giving him what I now had, and what he lacked."

Now they were three, a growing family, you might say. All because Mama stopped for the first one that day.

On they went through the market and the streets, stopping for the one to show them love's great feats.

Little Ellie and this young cheetah cub didn't have much,...

...except a little love.
But now they had a rising hope inside;...

...something they could whisper to those like them who had been tossed aside.

Their whispers spread through the market that day. One at a time, they had plenty to say.

"You are loved, a child of the King. Your life has more value than any of these things. I would like to call you one of our own, you belong to Papa God, His light and treasure inside you are what I've been shown."

35

And wouldn't you know, their family of three became an army of light, giving what they had to make others turn bright.

In a line they followed, more than fifty in tow, back to Mama's house for a family dinner did their growing troupe go.

A restful sleep they finally received, until morning came, and it was time for these little ones to go out towards the watering hole where they could impart more belief.

Together they redeemed monkeys who had lost their laugh...

And little zebras with faded stripes.

They watched wild wildebeests spring
to their feet...

And even the lion cub's once sad roar was suddenly, inexplicably restored.

So many little ones came back alive
with a new song, they just needed someone
to let them know it was Papa God to whom
they truly belong.

It started so simply, with a pause and a whisper, because one giraffe stopped to see a little elephants treasures, while others simply missed her.

She spoke an arrow of truth-filled love right to the heart, and hit the bulls eye of where new hope likes to start.

51

God's family grows one at a time, a word of heartfelt belief and encouragement upon which even the most broken can dine.

Because when you stop for the one who God places in your path, you'll always be right on time.

Joey and his wife, Destiny, have been married for 23 years. They have eight children and two grandchildren. As a family, they have both lived, and traveled, all around the world, empowering people to discover and live out who they were created to be. Joey has authored eleven books, and three children's books. As a family, they write and create to give life to a generation who will shine in the world.

To see other books and projects by the author, please visit: LeTourneau Creative

LeTourneau
Creative

LeTourneaucreative.com

www.ingramcontent.com/pod-product-compliance
Lightning Source LLC
Chambersburg PA
CBHW041431120626
46547CB00002B/176